GW00674930

FRANCIS FRITH'S

A Taste of

LINCOLNSHIRE
& THE FENS

REGIONAL RECIPES FROM LINCOLNSHIRE & THE FEN COUNTRY

Illustrated with historical photographs from
The Francis Frith Collection

FRANCIS FRITH'S

A Taste of
LINCOLNSHIRE
& THE FENS

Skegness, The Beach 1910 62867

Compiled by Julia Skinner

First published in the United Kingdom by
The Francis Frith Collection exclusively for Identity Books in 2009
Paperback Edition ISBN 978-1-84589-423-8

British Library Cataloguing in Publication Data

A Taste of Lincolnshire & The Fens
Julia Skinner

The Francis Frith Collection°
Frith's Barn, Teffont,
Salisbury, Wiltshire SP3 5QP
Tel: +44 (0) 1722 716 376
Email: info@francisfrith.co.uk
www.francisfrith.com

Printed and bound in Malta

Front Cover: Lincoln, The Strait c1955 L49083t
The colour-tinting in this image is for illustrative purposes only, and is not intended
to be historically accurate.

Every attempt has been made to contact copyright holders of illustrative material.
We will be happy to give full acknowledgement in future editions for any items not
credited. Any information should be directed to The Francis Frith Collection.

As with any historical database, the Francis Frith archive is constantly being
corrected and improved, and the publishers would welcome information on
omissions or inaccuracies.

CONTENTS

INTRODUCTION

Travel around Lincolnshire and the Fenland area through the pages of this book and discover a selection of the delicious traditional food of the region, as well as some of the stories and fascinating facts behind the recipes. Your journey will be given added savour by the historical images taken by photographers from The Francis Frith Collection, showing the people and places of this area in the past.

Regional traditional dishes were developed from the local produce that was available to thrifty housewives who had to feed large, hungry families on a limited budget. Many of the old recipes also reflect the limited cookery techniques that were available in the past, as well as the skills of the cooks who were able to provide cheap and tasty meals with only a fire, a skillet and a cauldron to cook with, often producing the historical version of 'boil in the bag' meals.

This book is not intended to provide a comprehensive collection of the local recipes of the region, and some recipes are modern interpretations using some of the fine local produce that the area is famous for, but we hope that the food described within these pages, as well as the descriptions of traditional customs, sayings and local dialect words, will provide you with a taste of Lincolnshire and the Fens.

Boston, A River View 1890 26067

SOUPS AND SNACKS

RECISPE

—·—

Pea Soup

Peas are cultivated on a large scale throughout Lincolnshire. Pea pods have an intense flavour, and this recipe ensures that this is not wasted.

> 450g/1 lb fresh peas in their pods
> 1 onion
> 50g/2oz butter
> 900ml/1½ pints good ham or vegetable stock
> 1 teaspoonful of sugar
> 2 sprigs of fresh mint
> 1 teaspoonful of cornflour
> 300ml/ ½ pint milk
> Salt and pepper

Shell the peas, wash the empty pods and remove the stringy edge and any other hard, fibrous bits. Peel and finely chop the onion. Melt the butter in a large heavy saucepan, add the peas, pods and chopped onion and fry gently for a few minutes until softened. Add the stock, sugar and sprigs of mint. Bring to the boil, then reduce heat, cover and simmer until the peas and pods are tender. Blend the cornflour with a little milk and stir it into the soup, together with the remaining milk. Increase the heat and bring the soup back to the boil, stirring all the time. Remove from heat and allow to cool for a few minutes, then liquidise the soup in a blender or pass it through a sieve. Season the soup with salt and pepper to taste, and reheat before serving.

—·—

The Quay Brewery

The Quay Brewery at Ely is on the right of this photograph. Beer has been brewed locally for at least 750 years; the monks at Ely once complained that their beer 'was so weak that the pigs would not drink of it'.

Ely, The River c1960 E34059

RECIPE

~ . ~

Celery and Stilton Soup

Celery is an important crop around Ely in Cambridgeshire, where it grows well in the rich, black Fenland soil.

40g/1½ oz butter
1 onion, finely chopped
1 potato, cut into small cubes
1 whole head of celery, thinly sliced
900ml/1½ pints good chicken or vegetable stock
115g/4oz Stilton cheese, crumbled
150ml/ ¼ pint single cream
Salt and freshly ground black pepper

Melt the butter in a large pan. Add the onion and cook over a medium heat for 5 minutes until it is transparent. Add the potato and celery and cook for a further 5 minutes until the vegetables begin to soften and brown. Add the stock, bring to the boil, then reduce heat, cover the pan and simmer for 30-40 minutes, until the vegetables are very soft. Allow to cool for a few minutes, then liquidise the soup in a blender, or pass it through a sieve, then return it to the pan and season to taste. Heat the soup through to just below the boil, then remove the pan from the heat, add the cheese and stir until it has melted. Stir in the cream and reheat just before serving, being careful not to allow the soup to boil.

~ . ~

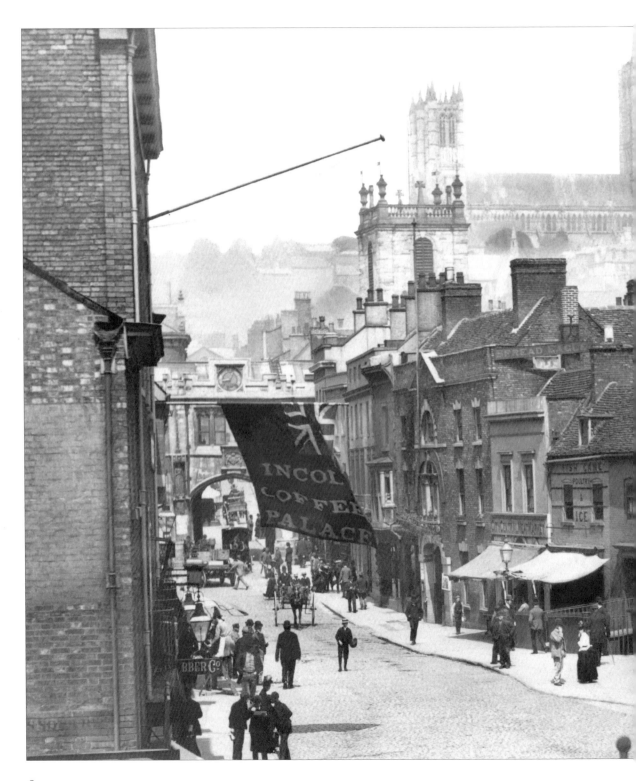

Lincoln, The Cathedral and Stonebow 1890 25654

Skegness, From the Pier 1910 62843

RECITE

~·~

North Coast Kipper Paté

2 boned kippers (or 4 kipper fillets)
1 tablespoonful double cream
115g/4oz softened butter
1 tablespoonful lemon juice
Cayenne pepper
¼ teaspoonful ground mace

Place the kippers, head down, into a jug, pour over enough boiling water to cover all but the tails and leave to stand for 5 minutes. Pour off the water and remove all skin and any small bones from the kippers, then set aside to cool.

Pound the kippers in a bowl with a wooden spoon until smooth, then blend in the cream, butter and lemon juice and season to taste with the cayenne pepper and ground mace. Spoon the paté into a small pot or dish, cover and refrigerate until required.

~·~

Scunthorpe 1904 52158v

Samphire

A wild plant called Marsh Samphire, or glasswort, is a delicacy found growing in salt marshes around the coast of Lincolnshire. The green fleshy tips of this succulent, bright green plant can be eaten raw or lightly cooked in salads, or hot with butter or with fish. A favourite way of preparing it is to boil the tips then simmer for 10 minutes, and then serve them with salt and plenty of vinegar. Samphire is in season from about the end of July, and should be collected by cutting it with scissors, not pulled up by the roots, so that it can grow again the next year. Samphire is often known as 'poor man's asparagus', but is also enjoyed by the rich – it was served at the royal wedding breakfast of Prince Charles and Lady Diana Spencer in 1981, as a symbol of Sandringham in Norfolk, where the royal family has a residence.

Skegness, Lumley Road 1899 44354

FISH

Grimsby, Fish Pontoon 1906 55750

Grimsby

By the 1920s Grimsby had grown into the largest and most prosperous fishing port in the world. A huge tonnage of cod, haddock and herring from the North Sea and the Icelandic fishing grounds was processed in the town to supply the length and breadth of the nation. During the inter-war years there was exceptional growth of the steam trawler fleets based in both Hull and Grimsby. These ships, with their port registration letters 'H' for Hull and 'G' for Grimsby, are seen in many of the photographs of the docks at this time. It is an astonishing fact that Grimsby alone, from this time and until the mid 1970s, provided one fifth of all the fish consumed in the UK. The eventual decline in the industry came as a result of the fishing limitations that Iceland placed on their fishing ground, which resulted in the aptly named 'cod wars' of the 1970s. The outcome was a huge decline in fish landings and the eventual loss of the deep sea trawling fleet – the Grimsby fishing industry was decimated. Fortunately though, Grimsby people adapt. Smaller shallow-water seine fishermen took over, and with a substantial fresh fish processing and cold storage facility in town, fish was still brought overland to Grimsby for sale and processing. The overall difference in fish tonnages passing through Grimsby is much reduced, but it has not spelt a death knell for the docks.

In recent years the Grimsby and Cleethorpes region has become one of the big commercial success stories, and the area has enjoyed unprecedented levels of inward investment. For several consecutive years the massive twin ports of Grimsby and Immingham have been confirmed as the largest and busiest ports in the UK. Internationally they are the sixth busiest port complex in Europe, whilst Immingham alone is the second busiest ferry terminal in the country. Over 10% of the nation's foodstuffs passes through the ports each day. Grimsby has set a standard as Europe's food capital, which keeps the docks especially alive and flourishing, and trade in Grimsby's £14 million state-of-the-art fish market is busy. Grimsby is now both the UK centre for buying, selling and freezing fish, and one of Europe's premier fishing and fish processing centres, with the largest frozen storage capacity in Europe. Appropriately for a place with such a strong fishing tradition, the multi-award-winning National Fishing Heritage Centre opened at the Alexandra Dock at Grimsby in 1991. The trawler 'Ross Tiger', which is moored outside the centre, is an excellent reminder of the proud heritage that built the town.

Grimsby, The Royal Dock c1955 G60019

RECIPE

Cod and Lime Fishcakes

This recipe is a reminder of Grimsby's deep-water fishing tradition.

750g/1½ lbs thick cod fillet
450g/1 lb large new potatoes, scrubbed and parboiled
Half an onion, grated
Zest of 1 lemon and 1 lime
Juice of 1 lime
Salt and freshly ground black pepper
2 tablespoonfuls sunflower oil

Place the cod fillet in a pan, and cover with water. Heat until the water simmers for 2 minutes, then turn off the heat, cover the pan and leave to cool. Alternatively the fish can be cooked in a microwave, covered with film, on a high setting for about 3 minutes, and then left to cool. When cooked and cooled, flake the fish into large pieces.

Grate the potatoes into a bowl, and add the flaked fish and grated onion, the lemon and lime zest and lime juice. Season with salt and freshly ground black pepper to taste. Shape the mix with your hands on a floured surface into 8 thick fishcakes, place them on a plate and leave to rest in the fridge for 10 minutes.

Heat the oil in a frying pan and fry the fish cakes on one side until they are crusty and browned, then turn them and cook the other sides.

RECIPE

—・—

North Sea Fisherman's Pie

In former years a fish pie was the traditional dish to be eaten at Easter, on Good Friday.

For the filling:
350ml/12 fl oz milk
1 bay leaf
Half an onion, finely sliced
450g/1 lb haddock or cod fillet
225g/8oz smoked haddock fillet
3 hard-boiled eggs, chopped
25g/1oz butter or margarine
25g/1oz plain flour
75g/3oz shelled prawns
2 tablespoonfuls chopped fresh parsley
Lemon juice to taste

For the topping:
500g /1¼ lbs potatoes, cooked
40g/1½ oz butter
60ml/ 4 tablespoonfuls milk
115g/4oz grated hard cheese of choice
Salt and pepper

Place the milk, the bay leaf and sliced onion in a saucepan over a medium heat and add the fish. Cover, and poach the fish lightly for 10 minutes. Strain, discard the bay leaf and reserve the milk for the sauce. Flake the fish into a buttered pie dish, discarding the skin and any remaining bones. Add the chopped eggs to the fish.

Melt 25g/1oz butter in a saucepan on a low heat, stir in the flour and cook gently for 1 minute, stirring continually. Remove the pan from the heat and stir in the reserved milk that the fish was poached in, a little at a time and stirring continually so that no lumps are formed. When all the milk has been mixed in, return the pan to the heat and bring the mixture to the boil, stirring continually as the sauce thickens, then simmer the sauce for about 4 minutes, still stirring all the time. Remove from the heat and stir in the prawns.

Add the parsley, lemon juice and seasoning to taste. Pour the sauce over the fish and eggs in the pie dish, and gently mix it all together.

Pre-heat the oven to 180°C/350°F/Gas Mark 4.

To make the topping
Gently heat 40g/1½ oz butter in 60ml/ 4 tablespoonfuls of milk in a small saucepan until the butter melts, then add the milk and melted butter to the cooked potatoes, mash and then beat until smooth. Spoon over the fish pie mixture to cover, then score the surface with a fork. Sprinkle the grated cheese over the pie before baking.

Bake the pie in the pre-heated oven for 25-30 minutes, until the top is golden.

—・—

Cleethorpes, The Beach 1906 55736

Skegness, The Beach 1910 62865

RECIPE

— . —

Herrings with Mustard Sauce

Herrings are highly nutritious and were a staple part of the diet in Victorian times. Here, the herrings are served with a savoury stuffing for a tasty lunch or supper. Mustard sauce is a traditional accompaniment to herrings in many parts of England.

4 large herrings	Mustard Sauce
3 heaped tablespoonfuls fresh white breadcrumbs	40g/1½ oz butter
	25g/1oz plain flour
1 heaped teaspoonful finely chopped parsley	450ml/ ¾ pint milk
	Salt and black pepper
A squeeze of lemon juice	1 level tablespoonful dry mustard powder
Grated rind of half a lemon	1 tablespoonful wine vinegar
Salt and black pepper	1 level teaspoonful caster sugar
Oil for frying	Lemon wedges and fresh parsley sprigs for garnish
25g/1oz butter	

Remove the heads from the herrings, clean, gut and bone them. Wash the herrings and pat them thoroughly dry. Put the breadcrumbs, parsley, lemon juice and lemon rind in a basin; season lightly with salt and freshly ground black pepper.

Melt the butter and stir into the breadcrumbs to bind the mixture, which should now be moist, but crumbly. Stuff the herrings with the breadcrumb mixture, and if necessary secure them with wooden cocktail sticks. Slash the skins crossways two or three times on each side; brush the herrings with oil and wrap each in foil. Put the herrings in a well-buttered deep baking dish; cover with lightly buttered greaseproof paper and bake in the centre of a pre-heated oven at 200°C/400°F/Gas Mark 6 for 35-40 minutes.

For the sauce, melt 25g/1oz of the butter in a pan; stir in the flour and cook for 1 minute. Gradually stir in the milk, beating well until the sauce is quite smooth. Bring to the boil and simmer for 2-3 minutes; season with salt and pepper. Blend the mustard powder with the vinegar and stir into the sauce; add the sugar. Check seasoning and stir in the remaining butter.

Transfer the baked herrings to a hot serving dish and garnish with wedges of lemon and sprigs of parsley. Serve the mustard sauce separately.

— . —

Peterborough, Market Square and Cathedral 1904 51544

RECIPE

Baked John Dory

Legend says that disaster followed the lighting of an oven in Peterborough in 1116, when a major fire destroyed the monastery buildings and the church. Traditionally the fire was said to have been caused when a monk, struggling to light the bake-house oven, cursed it and cried: 'Devil light the fire!' In 1118 work began on a new church, the present cathedral.

Peterborough's cathedral is dedicated to St Peter, St Paul and St Andrew. St Peter's feast day is 29th June. Hay-strewing ceremonies used to be common in many parts of the country on St Peter's Day, when fresh, sweet-smelling hay and rushes would be spread over the floors of churches; in some places parishioners would leave hayfields as bequests for the purpose of supplying Petertide hay for the church, providing a cheap and scented floor covering.

John Dory is often known as St Peter's fish – the black 'thumbprints' on each side of its head are said to be the marks of St Peter, who was a fisherman.

> 4 John Dory fillets
>
> 225g/8oz prawns
>
> 50g/2oz button mushrooms
>
> 1 teaspoonful anchovy essence
>
> 1 egg, beaten (optional)
>
> Salt and pepper
>
> 1 tablespoonful white wine or cider

Pre-heat the oven to 200°C/400°F/Gas Mark 6.

Wash the fish and wipe it dry. Cut into oblong strips. Finely chop the prawns and mushrooms, combine in a bowl and add the anchovy essence. Moisten, if necessary, with a little beaten egg. Put a little of this mixture on to each strip of fish and roll up into little parcels. Put into a buttered ovenproof dish, season with salt and pepper and moisten with the white wine or cider. Cover with buttered greaseproof paper and cook in the pre-heated oven for about 15 minutes, depending on the thickness of the fillets.

Eels

Eels were once so common in the fenland area of Cambridgeshire that they became a form of currency known as 'booklets' or 'sticks' of eels, with which land rent could be paid to the Church or State. One 'stick' comprised 25 eels. The monks at Ely exchanged 4,000 eels a year for the stone to build Ely Cathedral. Ironically, a local legend says that when the monastery at Ely was re-founded as a male religious house following the rule of St Benedict, after the destruction of an earlier religious house for women by marauding Danes in AD870, the monks were unwilling to embrace the newly imposed rule of celibacy, and were punished by being turned into eels!

Eels are still a local delicacy in Lincolnshire and the fenland area and smoked eels are well worth looking out for.

RECITE
— . —

Smoked Eel with Creamed Eggs

This makes a tasty breakfast dish.

> 225g/8oz smoked eel fillets
> 4 thinly sliced triangular pieces of white bread
> Oil for frying
> 8 eggs
> Salt and pepper
> 50g/2oz butter

Pre-heat the oven to 190°C/375°F/Gas Mark 5. Put the eel fillets in a small, shallow ovenproof dish, cover with foil and place in the pre-heated oven. Heat the oil in a frying pan and fry the bread triangles until they are golden brown on both sides, then drain on kitchen paper and keep hot.

Break the eggs into a bowl, season with salt and pepper and whisk lightly with a fork or balloon whisk. Melt the butter in a heavy-bottomed saucepan over a moderate heat. Pour in the eggs and cook gently, stirring all the time with a wooden spoon so that the eggs thicken gradually and do not go lumpy. When they are almost the consistency of lightly whipped cream, quickly remove the pan from the heat. Divide the eggs between four warmed plates, remove the eels from the oven and place two hot eel fillets on top of each serving of egg. Serve with triangles of fried bread on each plate.

— . —

Ely, The Cathedral c1878 10953

RECIPES

— . —

Eel Pie

1.4kg/3lbs skinned eels
300ml/ ½ pint fish stock
Salt and pepper
A pinch of mixed herbs
115g/4oz sliced onions
1 tablespoonful lemon juice
225g/8oz shortcrust pastry
1 egg

Cut the eels into small pieces and place them in a pan. Add the fish stock, salt and pepper, herbs and onions; simmer gently until the eel pieces are tender enough for the bones to be removed. Arrange the boned eels in a pie dish, and add the lemon juice and enough strained stock to cover the eels. Cover with pastry; brush with beaten egg and bake in a hot oven for about 45 minutes (225°C/425°F/Gas Mark 6). A little extra stock may be poured into the pie through a hole in the centre of the pastry before serving.

— . —

Fried Eels

450g/1 lb of skinned eels
1 beaten egg
A few breadcrumbs
Hot oil or lard for frying.

Wash the eels, cut them into pieces about 8cm (3 inches) long, trim and wipe them very dry; dredge with flour, brush the pieces with beaten egg, and cover with breadcrumbs; fry until nicely brown in the hot oil or lard. Garnish with fried parsley.

— . —

Fen Slodgers

This photograph shows a dredging barge being towed along the Great Ouse. The vital importance of maintaining the banks of Fenland rivers can clearly be seen in this photograph: notice how far below the level of the river are the houses on the extreme right. The men who carried out the drainage were known locally as 'Fen Slodgers'.

Littleport, The River c1955 L366006

Scunthorpe, Shops, Frodingham Road 1902 49011x

MEAT, POULTRY AND GAME

Louth, View from the Wolds c1955 L305014

RECIPE

~·~

Lincolnshire Beef Braised in Beer
with Herb Dumplings

The Lincoln Red is one of England's oldest beef breeds, producing a succulent meat with an excellent flavour. Use one of the many fine Lincolnshire-brewed beers to make this an even more authentic local dish.

For the stew:
25g/1oz butter
2 tablespoonfuls oil
115g/4oz streaky bacon, chopped into
    small pieces
900g/2 lbs Lincoln Red braising steak, cut
    into chunks
3 tablespoonfuls plain flour
450ml/ ¾ pint beer
450ml/ ¾ pint beef stock
1 bouquet garni

8 shallots or very small onions
175g/6oz button mushrooms
Salt and freshly ground black pepper

For the dumplings:
115g/4oz self-raising flour
50g/2oz shredded suet
Half a teaspoonful salt
Half a teaspoonful mustard powder
1 tablespoonful chopped fresh parsley
1 tablespoonful chopped fresh thyme

Melt half the butter with half the oil in a large heavy frying pan, add the bacon pieces and brown on both sides. Transfer the cooked bacon to a casserole dish. Brown the meat chunks in the frying pan in batches, a few pieces at a time, transferring them to the casserole when browned. Stir the flour into the remaining fat in the frying pan. Gradually add the beer and stock, stirring continually to mix it well together. Season to taste, then bring to the boil, constantly stirring as it thickens. Pour the sauce over the meat in the casserole dish and add the bouquet garni. Cover the casserole with its lid, and place it in a cold oven. Set the oven temperature to 200°C/400°F/Gas Mark 6. Cook for 30 minutes, then reduce the temperature to 160°C/325°F/Gas Mark 3 and cook for a further 1 hour.

Heat the remaining butter and oil in a frying pan and cook the shallots or onions until they are golden. Take the onions out of the pan, add the mushrooms and cook quickly for 2-3 minutes. Add the onions and mushrooms to the casserole and cook for a further 30 minutes, then make the dumplings.

Mix together the dumpling ingredients in a bow, then add enough cold water to form a soft dough. Flour your hands and roll the mixture into about 12 balls, and place them on top of the stew. Replace the casserole lid and cook the stew for 25-30 minutes more, then serve piping hot.

Grimsby Stocks

In former years Grimsby had three sets of stocks, two of which stood in the Bull Ring. They were used as a punishment for drunks and vagrants, and the Bull Ring stocks could admit two people simultaneously – both men and women could be punished in this way. The stocks were abolished by 1870. The last drunkard to be punished in the stocks was one Jack Mackinder; it was a cold and snowy day, and Mrs Emerson, a baker in the Bull Ring, kindly fed him a beefsteak pie dinner. For this exercise of charity, the mayor decreed she would be prosecuted for supplying a prisoner with food, but no punishment was ever meted out.

Grimsby, Bull Ring c1965 G60057

Lincolnshire Stuffed Chine

Stuffed chine is a speciality of Lincolnshire, a celebratory dish which was enjoyed at important events such as weddings and christenings and was also the traditional fare for May Day. The chine (a cut from the back of the pig) was cured for several weeks in salt and saltpetre, and then was slashed with a knife to form 'pockets' in the meat which were stuffed with whatever was to hand; although parsley was the most usual ingredient, lettuce, nettles, onion, sage, leeks, herbs and onion tops might also be used. The chine would then either be baked in a pastry case or tied up in a cloth and simmered for several hours.

In his book 'Hedingham Harvest', a chronicle of life in a (fictional) north Lincolnshire village in Victorian times, Geoffrey Robinson gave an evocative description of how his grandmother prepared her version of Lincolnshire stuffed chine, describing how she left the chine to stand for about a month for the salt and saltpetre to soak in. It was then hung for several more weeks. When it was dry, deep clefts would be cut in the chine which were stuffed with a mixture of finely chopped parsley, marjoram, thyme, chives and – most importantly – exactly 3 blackcurrant leaves. The rows of clefts filled with greenstuff gave the chine a striped appearance evocative of lines of crops sprouting in the fields in springtime. The chine was then baked in a pastry crust which was broken off and thrown away when the chine was ready for eating. The chine was always eaten cold, accompanied by an 'old-fashioned salad' made of lettuce leaves with chopped spring onions, sugar, salt and pepper, all of which was soaked in vinegar for an hour before eating.

Stamford, Market Place 1922 72298

RECITE

— . —

Lincolnshire Haslet

Lincolnshire Haslet (pronounced 'hacelet' locally) is a traditional meat loaf made with pork and seasoned with sage, unlike Welsh haslet which is made of liver.

175g/6oz pigs' liver

175g/6oz lean and fat bits of pork

75g/3oz pigs' heart

1 small onion

50g/2oz fresh breadcrumbs

2-3 leaves of fresh sage, chopped

1 teaspoonful salt

Pepper

Mince the liver, pork, heart and onion. Add the breadcrumbs and sage, and season with salt and pepper. Mix all together into a loaf shape, then wrap in foil and place on a small baking tray. Cook in a moderate oven, 180°C/350°F/Gas Mark 4, for about 1½ hours.

— . —

RECItPE

—·—

Toad in the Hole with Lincolnshire Sausages

Lincolnshire sausages are a distinctive variety of pork sausage that has a dominant flavour of herbs, with sage being the traditional flavouring. They are also notable for having an open, chunky texture, being made with pork that is coarsely ground, rather than minced.

> 450g/1 lb Lincolnshire sausages
> 175g/6oz plain flour
> A pinch of salt
> 2 eggs
> 600ml/1 pint milk and water mixed
> 15g/ ½ oz lard or dripping

Make the batter 1 hour before you start cooking the dish. Put the flour in a bowl with the salt, make a well in the centre and break in the eggs. Beat them into the flour, gradually adding the milk and water to make a smooth, creamy batter. Beat it well, then leave to stand for 1 hour. (This can also be prepared in a liquidiser.)

Pre-heat the oven to 220°C/425°F/Gas Mark 7.

Melt the lard or dripping in a frying pan and brown the sausages nicely all over (this gives a better flavour than cooking the sausages in the oven). Pour the fat and sausages into a 30cm (12 inch) roasting tin. Place the tin in the oven for a few minutes to heat through, then remove from the oven, pour in the prepared batter and replace the tin in the oven. When the batter is nicely puffed up , reduce the oven temperature to 190°C/375°F/Gas Mark 5, and continue cooking until well-risen and golden brown – the total cooking time from start to finish should be 35-40 minutes.

—·—

St Ives, Bridge Street 1898 41280

RECIPE

— · —

Hen on her Nest

1 chicken – 1.5kg/3 lbs
1 onion
2 carrots
1 teaspoonful of ground ginger
1 teaspoonful of mixed herbs
Salt and pepper
115g/4oz butter
225g/8oz long grain rice
4 eggs
50g/2oz flour
150ml/ ¼ pint double cream

Peel and slice the onion and carrots. Put the chicken, onion, carrots, mixed herbs, ginger, salt and pepper into a large saucepan. Add enough water to cover the chicken completely. Cover, and bring to the boil, then reduce heat and simmer for 2 hours. When cooked, transfer the chicken to a roasting tin, and retain the chicken stock.

Pre-heat the oven to 200°C/400°F/Gas Mark 6.

Spread half the butter over the skin of the chicken. Place the chicken in the pre-heated oven for 10 minutes to brown the skin. Remove from the oven and keep warm.

Whilst the chicken is cooking, hard-boil the eggs and shell them, and cook the rice: bring 600ml/1 pint of salted water to the boil. Put in the rice, stir, and bring back to the boil. Cover the pan, reduce heat and simmer for 20-25 minutes, or until the rice is cooked.

When the rice and chicken are cooked, make a roux with the flour and remaining butter, and cook for a few minutes. Gradually add 600ml/1 pint of the chicken stock and heat gently until the sauce thickens, stirring all the time. Remove from heat and stir in the cream.

Arrange the cooked rice on a plate and place the cooked chicken in the centre, with the hard-boiled eggs tucked underneath. Pour a little of the sauce over the chicken, and serve the rest separately.

— · —

Stamford, Horse and Carriage 1922 72316x

Bourne, North Street 1952 B511003

RECIPE

—·—

Traditional Roast Goose

In former centuries, geese were raised in great quantities in the eastern counties of England. In 1861 Mrs Beeton wrote: 'The best geese are found on the borders of Suffolk, and in Norfolk and Berkshire; but the largest flocks are reared in the fens of Lincolnshire and Cambridgeshire – large herds of them are sent every year to London'. In arable regions such as these, geese were fattened on stubble after the wheat harvest and then driven on foot in great droves to the London markets.

Legend says that Queen Elizabeth I received the news of the defeat of the Spanish Armada whilst she was eating goose on Michaelmas Day, and she ordained that thereafter this should be the traditional meal for Michaelmas. The calendar changes of 1752 officially moved Michaelmas Day to 29th September, but in parts of the country roast goose continued to be the traditional fare eaten for dinner on 'Old Michaelmas Day' (11th October). There was a saying that if you ate goose on this day, you would not want for money for the following year:

'Whoever eats goose on Michaelmas Day
Shall never lack money for his debts to pay.'

1 goose
115g/4oz pork
115g/4oz veal
1 large onion
A small knob of butter
2 slices of bread soaked in milk
1 egg yolk
Parsley, thyme, sage, finely chopped
3fl oz/75ml red wine

Make a stuffing by chopping the pork, veal, onion and the goose liver very finely and brown them in the butter. Squeeze the milk out of the bread and mix together all the ingredients except the wine, and using only a little of the wine to moisten. Season with salt and pepper to taste. Stuff the goose with the mixture and put it into a very hot oven, about 230°C/450°F/Gas Mark 8, for 15 minutes. Reduce the heat to 180°C/350°F/Gas Mark 4, and cook for a further 15 minutes per 450g/1 lb weight of the goose, basting with the remaining wine and juices in the roasting dish.

—·—

RECIPE

— . —

Roast Wild Duck

The Fens are particularly known for the variety of wildfowl to be found there. Both wild duck and geese formed an important part of the local diet in past times. Wild duck, such as mallard, teal and widgeon, should not be overcooked – allow a roasting time of between 30-50 minutes, depending on the size of the bird.

> 1 wild duck
> A knob of butter
> Orange juice
>
> For the sauce:
> 1 tablespoonful of lemon juice
> 1 tablespoonful of sugar
> 2 tablespoonfuls of port wine
> 1 tablespoonful of tomato ketchup
> Salt
> Cayenne pepper

Pre-heat the oven to 190°C/375°F/Gas Mark 5.

Put the duck in a roasting tin. Place a knob of butter inside the duck, and pour some orange juice over the bird. Roast in the pre-heated oven for about 30-50 minutes (depending on the size of the bird) until it is tender, basting occasionally with the juices in the tin. When the duck is cooked, mix all the sauce ingredients together and pour over the bird before serving.

— . —

Grantham, Westgate 1904 51631

CHEESE AND VEGETABLE DISHES

Spalding, In the Bulb Fields c1955 S388193

RECITE

— • —

Cabbage and Bacon

Lincolnshire is famous for growing spring bulbs and early vegetables in the flat fertile fields of much of the county. It is a major producer of barley, wheat and sugar beet, but peas, cabbages, cauliflowers and onions are also important crops.

> 1 large crisp white cabbage
> 4 rashers of back bacon
> 4 rashers of streaky bacon
> A knob of butter
> Salt, pepper and a pinch of ground allspice

Trim and quarter the cabbage and wash it well. Bring a large pan of salted water to the boil and add the cabbage. While it is cooking, cut the bacon into small pieces, and fry in butter in a hot frying pan. When it is tender, after about 10 minutes, drain the cabbage thoroughly, cut it into shreds with a knife and press lightly to strain off the water. Place it in a mound on a deep dish and throw the bacon and its hot fat over the top. Season with pepper and a pinch of allspice.

— • —

RECITE

—·—

Stuffed Onions with Lincolnshire Poacher Cheese

Lincolnshire Poacher Cheese, made by F W Read and Sons, is an unpasteurised cheese that is handmade from a traditional recipe only between the months of October and May. It is matured for an exceptionally long time – 15 to 18 months – to produce a flavoursome, full bodied cheese which was judged to be of Gold Medal standard at the British Cheese Awards in 2001.

4 large onions
50g/2oz fresh breadcrumbs
50g/2oz bacon, finely chopped
1 teaspoonful of sage, finely chopped
Salt and pepper to taste
25g/1oz butter
25g/1oz grated Lincolnshire Poacher cheese
A little chopped fresh parsley to garnish

Remove the onion skins, but keep the onions whole. Place the onions in a large pan of boiling water, and boil for 20 minutes until they are softened.

Pre-heat the oven to 200°C/400°F/Gas Mark 6.

Remove the onions from the pan and drain, then leave to cool for a few minutes. Cut the top of each onion, then scoop out the centre and finely chop. Mix together the chopped cooked onions, breadcrumbs, bacon and sage, and season to taste, then mix in the butter well. Use the mixture to fill each onion shell, and sprinkle the tops with the grated cheese. Stand the onions on a baking tray, and bake in the pre-heated oven for about 30 minutes. Serve garnished with the chopped parsley.

—·—

RECIPE

Celery Baked in Cream

Carrots and celery thrive around Ely, and more than half of the British outdoor crop of celery comes from this area. This is a famous local recipe where the use of a little cream brings out the flavour of the celery. It is an excellent accompaniment to meat or fish.

1 large head of celery, washed and trimmed
¼ teaspoonful of ground allspice
2 garlic cloves, skinned and crushed
300ml/10 fl oz fresh single cream
Salt and pepper
25g/1oz fresh wholemeal breadcrumbs

Pre-heat the oven to 200°C/400°F/Gas Mark 6.

Reserve a few celery leaves to garnish, then cut the celery sticks lengthways into thin strips. Cut each strip into 5cm (2 inch) lengths and put them into a greased ovenproof serving dish. Mix the ground allspice with the crushed garlic and cream, season to taste, and pour over the celery in the dish. Sprinkle with the breadcrumbs. Bake in the pre-heated over for about 1¼ hours or until the celery is tender, then serve hot, garnished with the reserved celery leaves.

St Ives, Sheep Market 1931 84547

PUDDINGS, PIES AND DESSERTS

St Ives, Farmworkers 1931 84558x

RECIPE

Lincolnshire Potato Cheesecake

This was traditionally served at Harvest Home suppers.

First put the potatoes on to cook and while they are cooking make the pastry – steamed or pressure cooked potatoes are best, but otherwise boil them.

For the pastry:
175g/6oz soft plain flour
40g/1½ oz butter or margarine
40g/1½ oz lard
A pinch of salt
3 full dessertspoonfuls of cold water

Rub the fats into the flour and salt until the mixture resembles fine breadcrumbs. Mix to a firm dough with the water, and do not be tempted to add more water. Knead the dough lightly until it is smooth and pliable. Roll out on a floured board. Use the pastry to line an 18-20cm (7- 8 inch) round flan tin. Prick all over the pastry on the base of the tin with a fork. Leave to rest while mixing the filling.

For the filling:
225g/8oz hot cooked potatoes
A pinch of salt
A pinch of nutmeg
115g/4oz softened butter or margarine
115g/4oz caster sugar
2 eggs, well-beaten
Grated rind and juice of 1 lemon

Pre-heat the oven to 200°C/400°F/Gas Mark 6.

Sieve the hot potatoes with the salt and nutmeg. Add the butter or margarine, sugar, eggs, the grated lemon rind and the lemon juice. Beat thoroughly together. Fill the pastry-lined flan tin almost to the top with the mixture. Place the flan tin on a baking tray and bake in the pre-heated oven on the middle shelf for 15 minutes, then remove the potato cake from the flan tin, place on the baking tray and bake for a further 10 more minutes until the filling is set and browning on top.

Boston, Market Place 1899 43295

Lincolnshire Dialect Words

'Frim folk' - people from another area.

'Reasty' - rancid.

'Chunter' - to complain.

'Starnil' - a starling.

'Kecks' - trousers.

'Mardy' - bad tempered, sulky.

'Kelch' - mud.

'Wick' - lively.

'Wassack' or 'Gump' - a fool.

'Jiffle' - fidget.

'Yucker' - a young person.

'Throng' - busy.

'Uneppen' - clumsy.

'Proggle' - to poke about (with a stick).

Queen Vic's Coronation Dinner

On 28th June 1838, the Market Place of Wisbech in Cambridgeshire played host to a memorable event: a dinner in honour of Queen Victoria's coronation. This saw 5,000 people regaled, at a cost of £408, with nearly 300 stones of roast beef, 260 stones of potatoes and 542 plum puddings – weighing 7 pounds each. The feast was followed by rustic sports including 'jinglin' matches and a tea drinking competition for women of 40 years and above. There was a balloon ascent and the event concluded with a fireworks display. Similar dinners were held for Victoria's two jubilees and Edward VII's coronation, the latter event being followed by a tea for 3,500 of the town's schoolchildren.

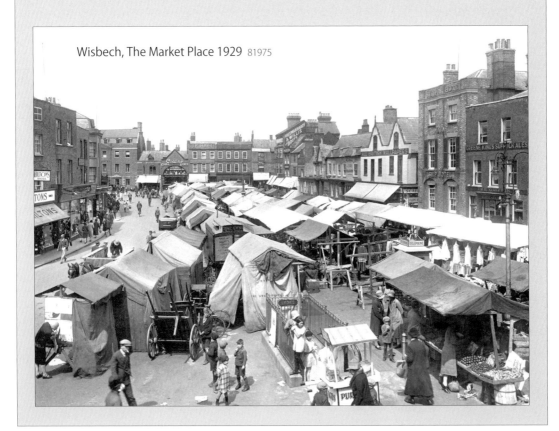

Wisbech, The Market Place 1929 81975

RECIPE

—.—

Summer Pudding

Wisbech in Cambridgeshire is often referred to as 'the capital of the Fens'. From the end of the 19th century, the fruit industry around Wisbech started to develop in earnest, and the town and district began to gain a reputation as a centre for the production of high quality fruits, such as strawberries, gooseberries, apples, pears etc. All this soft fruit is ideal for making Summer Pudding.

> 10 slices of crustless white bread – use bread from a proper loaf, not a sliced and wrapped one, for best results
>
> 3 tablespoonfuls of milk
>
> 750g/1½ lbs soft fruit – use a variety of such fruits as raspberries, cherries, redcurrants, blackcurrants, white currants, loganberries or (sparingly) strawberries
>
> 115g/4oz caster sugar

Reserve a few pieces of fresh fruit to decorate. Lightly butter a pudding basin of 1 litre/1¾ pint capacity. Moisten the bread with milk. Hull, stone or top and tail the fruit as necessary. Cook it all very gently in the sugar for 4-5 minutes until the sugar melts and the juices run. Spoon off a few spoonfuls of the juice as it cools and reserve.

Line the sides and bottom of the pudding basin with the bread slices, cutting them to fit where necessary and checking that there are no spaces. Reserve enough bread slices for a lid. Pour in the fruit, which should come almost to the top, and cover closely with the remaining bread. Put a small plate over the top (it should just fit inside the rim of the basin), and weight it with something heavy. Leave to press overnight in the fridge.

To serve, remove the weight and the plate. Place a deep serving dish over the top of the pudding basin and reverse quickly so that the pudding comes out easily in one piece. Pour the remaining juices slowly all over the pudding, especially over the places where the juice has not seeped through thoroughly. Keep cold.

—.—

Wisbech, The Clarkson Memorial 1901 47583

RECIPE

～·～

Apple Dowdy

The Wisbech area is known for its soft fruit, but is also famous for its acres of apple orchards, where the Bramley apple in particular is widely grown.

Juice of half a lemon
300ml/ ½ pint water
675g/1½ lbs cooking apples, peeled, cored and sliced
About 6 slices of stale bread, buttered
Grated nutmeg
50g/2oz golden syrup
25g/1oz soft brown sugar

Pre-heat the oven to 180°C/350°F/Gas Mark 4.

Put the water and lemon juice into a bowl, add the sliced apples and leave for a few minutes. Line a greased pie dish with the buttered bread, buttered sides in, cutting them to fit where necessary, and reserving enough slices to make a 'lid'. Drain the apples and arrange them in the pie dish, sprinkling them with a little grated nutmeg.

Gently heat the golden syrup and 1 tablespoonful of water in a small saucepan until the syrup is thin and runny, then pour it over the apples, and sprinkle them with the brown sugar. Cover the apples with a layer of the reserved buttered bread.

Cover the pie dish with foil and bake in a pre-heated oven for 45 minutes to 1 hour, until the apples are soft. Serve hot with cream.

～·～

RECIPE

— · —

Plum Pudding

King's Lynn is a major port of the Fenland region. St Ann's Fort, off North Street in the town, is now just a square beside the port offices. It was built as a gun battery protecting the river in 1570, and re-armed in 1626. Guns were replaced here with each threat of war, and stood from 1778 to the 1830s. In 1778 the Lynn volunteers joined by reciting an oath beginning 'That you will always prefer roast beef, plum pudding and good English beer, to soup maigre, fricassed frog and French wines . . .'.

> 115g/4oz fresh breadcrumbs
> 115g/4oz plain flour
> 115g/4oz suet
> 115g/4oz soft brown sugar
> 1 heaped teaspoonful of baking powder
> 115g/4oz mixed dried fruit
> 1 teaspoonful ground mixed spice
> A small amount of milk, to mix

Put all the ingredients in a bowl and mix well, adding enough milk to form a stiff dough.

Sprinkle a clean pudding cloth or tea towel with a little flour. Shape the dough into a thick roll and place on the cloth, leaving a pleat of material at each end. Roll up the dough in the cloth and tie each end securely with string, and also tie it loosely around the centre to help the pudding keep its shape. Put the pudding into a large pan of boiling water and boil for 1½ hours, topping up the pan with more boiling water when necessary – take care not to allow it to boil dry. When the pudding is cooked, remove it from the pan, cut the string and remove the cloth and turn out the pudding onto a warmed dish. Serve with cream or custard, and also a little golden syrup if liked.

— · —

Tickler's Artillery

In 1879 a Mr T G Tickler of Grimsby, who had a fondness for fine jam, despaired at the quality of shop-bought jam and set about making his own in premises on Cleethorpes Road. Twenty years later, after moving to Hope Street and then Pasture Street, he followed his success with the management of his own orchards on a 230-acres estate at Bradley village on the town's outskirts. Having enjoyed success from selling large amounts of jam to the government for Boer War troops, he had similar success providing jam for First World War soldiers. Tickler's jam was doubly useful in the First World War, for once the contents of the tins were consumed, the empty tins made excellent hand grenades when they were refilled with explosives. They were known colloquially as 'Tickler's Artillery'. At its peak, Tickler's had further factories in Middlesex and Scotland, and controlled the Lincoln Preserving Co Ltd and the Crosbie Pure Food Co Ltd. Their star product was Nell Gwynn marmalade. The company continued into the 1970s until it was finally bought out and closed by Robertson Foods Ltd.

King's Lynn, The Custom House 1898 40878

RECIPE

—·—

Apple Florentine Pie

This dish was traditionally made at Christmas in Lincolnshire.

4 large cooking apples	For the shortcrust pastry:
3 tablespoonfuls demerara sugar	¼ teaspoonful salt
1 tablespoonful grated lemon peel	225g/8oz plain flour
50g/2oz sultanas	115g/4oz butter or margarine
600ml/1 pint pale ale	50ml/2 fl oz very cold water
¼ teaspoonful grated nutmeg	
¼ teaspoonful cinnamon	
3 cloves	
Whipped cream, to serve	

Oven temperature: 200°C/400°F/Gas Mark 6.

Make the pastry by mixing the salt and flour lightly together and rubbing in the butter or margarine until the mixture resembles fine breadcrumbs. Mix with the cold water until a soft dough is formed. Roll out to 1cm (½ inch thick) on a floured board.

Peel and core the apples, stand them in a deep, buttered ovenproof pie dish and sprinkle with 2 tablespoonfuls of the sugar and 1 teaspoonful of the grated lemon peel. Fill the centre of each apple with sultanas. Cover the dish with the pastry and bake in the pre-heated oven for 30 minutes.

Heat together, but do not boil, the ale, nutmeg, cinnamon, cloves and remaining sugar. Remove the pie dish from the oven, carefully loosen the pastry crust and lift the pastry off the apples. Pour the ale mixture over the apples. Put each apple into a bowl, cut the pastry into 4 pieces and place one piece on top of each apple. Serve very hot, with whipped cream.

—·—

Jelly Junket

In 1506 the Guild of St Mary in Boston sent a deputation to Rome to try to get more privileges for their members from Pope Julius II. They were advised that the best way to get the Pope's attention was to approach him as he came back from hunting. They sang a three-man glee, and then offered him a 'Jelly Junket', which was a sort of sweet pudding. They were successful, and got 500 years of pardon for those members of their guild whose subscriptions were paid up.

Boston, Shodfriars Hall 1889 22274

Skegness, The Beach 1910 62867

RECIPE

— . —

Lincolnshire Carrot Pudding

This Lincolnshire recipe for a fruity steamed pudding makes a good light alternative to a traditional Christmas Pudding.

> 115g/4oz plain flour
> 115g/4oz shredded suet
> 115g/4oz raisins
> 115g/4oz currants
> 115g/4oz grated raw potato
> 115g/4oz grated raw carrot
> 115g/4oz demerara sugar
> 115g/4oz fresh breadcrumbs
> ½ teaspoonful bicarbonate of soda
> 1 teaspoonful ground mixed spice
> 25g/1oz chopped glace cherries
> 1 large egg (beaten)
> A little milk for mixing, if necessary

In a large bowl, mix together the flour, bicarbonate of soda and mixed spice. Add all the other dry ingredients and mix it all well together. Add the beaten egg and mix it in to bind the mixture, adding a little milk if necessary. Put the mixture into a large, greased pudding basin, making sure that space is left at the top as the mixture will expand during cooking. Cover the basin with a double layer of pleated greaseproof paper and a piece of foil, and tie down firmly with string.

Place the pudding basin in a large saucepan of boiling water and cover with the saucepan lid. Steam for 3 hours, topping up the saucepan with more boiling water from time to time to ensure that the pan does not boil dry.

When cooked, turn out the pudding onto a warm serving dish and serve piping hot, with custard, cream or brandy sauce.

— . —

Scunthorpe, High Street 1904 52160v

TEATIME AND BAKING

Market Rasen, Town Hall Cinema c1955 M231002

RECITE

— . —

Lincolnshire Plum Bread

'Plum' in recipes usually means dried fruit such as currants, raisins and sultanas, but in this recipe plums are indeed used, albeit in their dried form as prunes. This is especially good if the dried fruit is soaked overnight in cold (milkless) tea before cooking.

450g/1 lb plain flour (strong breadmaking flour is best)
225g/8oz prunes, cut into small pieces
115ml/4fl oz milk, warm
115g/4oz butter, melted
4 tablespoonfuls caster sugar
50g/2oz currants
50g/2oz sultanas
15g/ ½ oz easy-blend dried yeast
2 eggs, lightly beaten
1 teaspoonful ground cinnamon
1 teaspoonful ground allspice
1 pinch of salt

Mix together the milk, sugar, butter, yeast, beaten egg, salt, and spices. Add the flour, and beat the mixture until it is smooth, to make soft pliable dough. Turn out the dough onto a floured surface, and knead it until it is smooth and elastic. Place the dough in a bowl, cover, and allow the bowl to stand in a warm place until the dough has doubled in size.

Knock back the dough and knead it again briefly, adding the dried fruit and making sure that it is evenly distributed. Divide the dough into two pieces, and place into two 450g (1 lb) greased and lined loaf tins. Cover and leave again in a warm place rise until doubled in size.

Pre-heat the oven to 190°C/375°F/Gas Mark 5.

Place the loaf tins on a pre-heated baking sheet and bake for 40-50 minutes, then remove the loaves from the tins and return them to the oven to cook for a further 5-10 minutes, or until they sound hollow when tapped on the base. Store the loaves in an airtight container and serve in slices, spread with butter. This also makes excellent toast.

— . —

Crowland, The Abbey c1955 C198007a

RECITE

— · —

Grantham Gingerbread Balls

In the south-east of Lincolnshire, the town of Grantham is famous for a special type of gingerbread. The recipe is said to have been devised by mistake when a local baker in the 1740s was making Grantham Whetstones, a type of flat hard biscuits, and added the wrong ingredients to the mixture. Unlike other gingerbreads, the Grantham version does not contain black treacle and so is known as a 'white' gingerbread. Traditionally the ginger flavour is strong, so use as much ginger as you prefer.

> 450g/1 lb plain flour
> 450g/1 lb caster sugar
> 225g/8oz butter
> 1 egg, beaten
> 1 teaspoonful baking powder
> Half a teaspoonful bicarbonate of soda
> 1-2 level teaspoonfuls ground ginger, to taste

Pre-heat the oven to 160°C/300°F/Gas Mark 2.

In a large bowl, cream the butter, gradually adding the sugar, and beat until light and fluffy. Stir the beaten egg into the mixture. Gradually fold in the sieved flour, bicarbonate of soda, baking powder and ground ginger to the mixture.

Form the mixture into small balls and flatten each on to ungreased baking sheets. Bake in the pre-heated over for 20 minutes or until they are light brown – do not let them cook until they are very dark. This recipe makes about 50-60 gingerbread balls.

— · —

Grantham, Vine Street 1890 27851

RECIPE

— . —

Lincolnshire Farmhouse Dripping Cake

225g/8oz plain flour
Half a level teaspoonful of salt
175g/6oz dripping
50g/2oz candied peel, chopped
225g/8oz raisins
175g/6oz sugar
1 tablespoonful of black treacle
Approx 300ml/ ½ pint of milk
2 eggs, beaten
1 level teaspoonful of bicarbonate of soda

Pre-heat the oven to 180°C/350°F/Gas Mark 4.

Grease an 18-20cm (8 inch) square cake tin and line with greaseproof paper. Sift the flour with the salt, rub in the dripping. Add chopped candied peel, raisins and sugar to the flour. Warm the treacle in half of the milk, mix with the eggs and add to the ingredients in the bowl. Dissolve the bicarbonate of soda in 1 tablespoonful of the milk and add. Stir all together using the remaining milk as necessary to make a consistency that will just drop from the spoon when it is shaken. Put into prepared cake tin. Level the top with the back of a spoon. Bake in the pre-heated moderate oven for 1½ - 2 hours. Reduce temperature to 160°C/325°F/Gas Mark 3 after one hour.

— . —

Stamford, Children by the River 1922 72296x

RECITE

—·—

Fen Country Apple Cake

750g/1½ lbs cooking apples

Juice of half a lemon

25g/1oz butter or margarine

50g/2oz caster sugar

2 rounded tablespoonfuls of semolina

225g/8oz shortcrust or puff pastry

25g/1oz currants

3 tablespoonfuls of black treacle

Peel, core and slice the apples. Put the apples, lemon juice and butter into a pan, cover, and simmer slowly until pulpy. Add the sugar and semolina, and bring slowly to the boil. Cook gently for five minutes or until the mixture has thickened. Remove from the heat and leave until completely cold. Divide the pastry into two pieces. Roll out one portion and use to line an 18-20cm (7-8 inch) heatproof pie plate. Spread with half the apple filling to within half an inch of the edges. Sprinkle with currants and add the treacle, and then top with the remaining filling. Roll out the rest of the pastry into a 22-24cm (8-9 inch) round, moisten the edges with water and cover the pie. Press the edges well together to seal, and knock up with the back of a knife. Brush the top with beaten egg or milk and then bake towards the top of the oven at 220°C/425°F/Gas Mark 7 for 25-30 minutes or until pale gold in colour.

—·—

Peterborough, The Butter Cross 1890 24451

RECINE

—·—

Lincoln Ginger Biscuits

350g/12oz self-raising flour
225g/8oz sugar
2 teaspoonfuls bicarbonate of soda
115g/4oz butter or margarine
2 teaspoonfuls ground ginger
2 teaspoonfuls golden syrup
1 beaten egg

Place all the dry ingredients in a bowl. Heat the butter or margarine and golden syrup gently in a pan until the fat has melted, then pour over the dry ingredients and mix to a fairly stiff consistency, whilst slowly adding in the beaten egg. Roll small pieces of the dough in your hand to make balls about the size of a walnut.

Place each ball of dough on a greased baking sheet, making sure they are well spaced apart. Bake for 15-20 minutes at 180°C/350°F/Gas Mark 4 until golden brown.

—·—

Alford, The Mill c1955 A209026

RECITE

—.—

Fourses Cake

This traditional lardy bread was served to harvesters in the afternoons, together with a sweetened beer known as 'sugar beer'. It was probably named 'fourses' because it was served at the four o'clock break, although the name may also relate to the custom of marking the bread into four sections which was followed in some areas.

675g/1½ lbs strong plain flour
1 level teaspoonful salt
2 teaspoonfuls ground mixed spice
175g/6oz lard, softened
15g/ ½ oz dried yeast
2 teaspoonfuls sugar
450ml/ ¾ pint warm water
175g/6oz currants
A little milk to glaze

Mix the yeast with the sugar and a little of the warmed water, and keep in a warm place until it has frothed up.

Sift the flour, salt and spice into a bowl. Rub in the lard and add the creamed yeast mixture. Stir in the remaining water and mix to a smooth, pliable dough. Knead the dough thoroughly, then cover the bowl with a cloth and leave to rise in a warm place until the dough has doubled in size. Knock back, and knead in the currants.

Either shape the dough into loaves and put into 450g/1 lb loaf tins, or shape it in to a large round and place on a greased baking sheet, and leave to rise again. If you are making the round loaf version, it is now traditional to mark the top of the loaf into four sections with a sharp knife.

Brush the top with milk to glaze, and bake in a hot oven (200°C/400°F/Gas Mark 6) for 45 minutes, until well risen and golden brown.

—.—

Cleethorpes, Flying Machine 1906 55735

Lincoln, Stonebow 1901 46773

INDEX OF PHOTOGRAPHS

INDEX OF RECIPES

Peterborough, Westgate 1904 51550

FREE PRINT OF YOUR CHOICE

Mounted Print
Overall size 14 x 11 inches (355 x 280mm)

Choose any Frith photograph in this book.
Simply complete the Voucher opposite and
return it with your remittance for £3.50 (to cover
postage and handling) and we will print the
photograph of your choice in SEPIA (size 11 x 8
inches) and supply it in a cream mount with a
burgundy rule line (overall size 14 x 11 inches).
Please note: aerial photographs and
photographs with a reference number
starting with a "Z" are not Frith photographs
and cannot be supplied under this offer.
Offer valid for delivery to one UK address only.

PLUS: **Order additional Mounted Prints
at HALF PRICE - £9.50 each** (normally £19.00)
If you would like to order more Frith prints from
this book, possibly as gifts for friends and family,
you can buy them at half price (with no
additional postage and handling costs).

PLUS: **Have your Mounted Prints framed**
For an extra £18.00 per print you can have your
mounted print(s) framed in an elegant polished
wood and gilt moulding, overall size
16 x 13 inches (no additional postage and
handling required).

IMPORTANT!

These special prices are only available if you use
this form to order. You must use the ORIGINAL
VOUCHER on this page (no copies permitted). We
can only despatch to one UK address. This offer
cannot be combined with any other offer.

Send completed Voucher form to:
**The Francis Frith Collection, Frith's Barn,
Teffont, Salisbury, Wiltshire SP3 5QP**

CHOOSE A PHOTOGRAPH FROM THIS BOOK

Voucher *for* **FREE** *and Reduced Price Frith Prints*

*Please do not photocopy this voucher. Only the original is valid,
so please fill it in, cut it out and return it to us with your order.*

Picture ref no	Page no	Qty	Mounted @ £9.50	Framed + £18.00	Total Cost £
		1	Free of charge*	£	£
			£9.50	£	£
			£9.50	£	£
			£9.50	£	£
			£9.50	£	£
			£9.50	£	£

*Please allow 28 days
for delivery.
Offer available to one
UK address only*

* Post & handling	£3.50
Total Order Cost	£

Title of this book . . . .

I enclose a cheque/postal order for £ . . . .

made payable to 'The Francis Frith Collection'

OR please debit my Mastercard / Visa / Maestro card,
details below

Card Number

Issue No (Maestro only)   Valid from (Maestro)

Expires   Signature

Name Mr/Mrs/Ms . . . .

Address . . . .

. . . .

. . . .

. . . . Postcode . . . .

Daytime Tel No . . . .

Email . . . .

978-1-84589-423-8   Valid to 31/12/11

Can you help us with information about any of the Frith photographs in this book?

We are gradually compiling an historical record for each of the photographs in the Frith archive. It is always fascinating to find out the names of the people shown in the pictures, as well as insights into the shops, buildings and other features depicted.

If you recognize anyone in the photographs in this book, or if you have information not already included in the author's caption, do let us know. We would love to hear from you, and will try to publish it in future books or articles.

An Invitation from The Francis Frith Collection to Share Your Memories

The 'Share Your Memories' feature of our website allows members of the public to add personal memories relating to the places featured in our photographs, or comment on others already added. Seeing a place from your past can rekindle forgotten or long held memories. Why not visit the website, find photographs of places you know well and add YOUR story for others to read and enjoy? We would love to hear from you!

www.francisfrith.com/memories

Our production team

Frith books are produced by a small dedicated team at offices in the converted Grade II listed 18th-century barn at Teffont near Salisbury, illustrated above. Most have worked with the Frith Collection for many years. All have in common one quality: they have a passion for the Frith Collection.

Frith Books and Gifts

We have a wide range of books and gifts available on our website utilising our photographic archive, many of which can be individually personalised.

www.francisfrith.com